Intuitive Insights

Perceptions of a Pensive Mind

Dr Naren Kumar Reddy Telluri

BookLeaf Publishing

India | USA | UK

Made with ❤ on the BookLeaf Publishing Platform
www.bookleafpub.in
www.bookleafpub.com

Dedication

" Dedicated to my dad, Siva Sesha Reddy; my mom, Koteswari; my brother, Pavan Kumar Reddy; my sister-in-law Mounika; my darling niece, Srikruthi; my wife, Dr Teja Sri; our baby Berry and my senior, Dr Amulya who always believed in me. Amy Rees Anderson always said, 'A person who feels appreciated will always do more than expected'

Preface

Intuitive Insights is a collection of perceived intuitions that provoke deep thought. Emotions drive the heart, leading to questions about its existential nature based on real experiences.

Acknowledgements

I appreciate every person who has crossed my path, whether for good or bad, as they have all provoked my intuitive thoughts. Writing became a part of my life in a way I never imagined, even in my wildest dreams. There was a time when I felt overwhelmed with thoughts as if my mind would explode unless I put them on paper. Every encounter with different persons during that period impacted me, prompting me to think, reflect, construct and create ideas that flowed into words, bringing me immense solace. From that point forward, writing became a routine for me. Without those experiences and connections, this book would not exist.

1. Focus

Focus on light in the darkness
Focus on strengths in weakness
Focus on comfort when in pain
Focus on smiles in despair
Focus on positivity in negativity
Focus on breathing when it's hard to breathe
Focus on living while struggling to live
Focus on working in confusion
Focus is all we need to survive
Focus on truth in falsity
Focus is all we need
Focus on what we are supposed to do rather than what
we should have done
Focus on living rather than how we should be living
Focus on loving rather than how we should be loved
Focus on caring rather than how we should be cared
Focus on being kind rather than being rude or lecturing
on kindness
Focus on life before dying
Focus on being clear about what we want

Focus on clarity in life

Look at the bigger and farther picture of life; we are always a step away from clarity.

2. Give Up

Give up
Give up the fear. Give up the scare.
Give up the pride. Give up the chide.
Give up the anger. Give up the danger.
Give up the heat. Give up the beat.
Give up the pain. Give up the tear.
Give up the rumour. Give up the sober.
Give up the give-ups
So much to give up, So much to gain
Never give up on yourself
Never give up on hope.
Never give up on time.
Never give up on life !!
Never give up on love.
Never give up on caring.
Never give up on being kind.
Never give up on you !!!

3. Limits

Limited by the limits of the mind
Limited by the limits of responsibility
Limited by the limits of conscience
Limited by the limits of tranquillity
Limited by the limits of liberty
Limited by the limits of bandage
Limited by the limits of language
Limited by the limits of the challenge
Limited by the limits of change
Life is limited by the limits created by the thoughts
Life is limitless in the way you create, innovate, invent
Let the limits never define the impact you can create
Let the limits never define the ripple you can reverberate
Limits are limited

4. Emotions

Life is an emotional tornado
We go through many emotions
We grow through many emotions
We live the emotion
We live through the emotion
We shape around emotions
We shape through emotions
So many emotions. So much turmoil
So many feelings, So much guile
We feel till the threshold is reached.
We think till the bag is full.
From then on, every emotion, every feeling
will overflow without any impact
It's just like striking a deadlog!!!

5. Life I live

I live in a world Where I have to reassure myself that I
am alive
I live in a world Where I have to reassure myself that I
am okay
I live in a world Where I have to reassure myself that I
am strong
I live struggling to find my feet.
I live struggling to find my voice
I live struggling to find my heart
I live struggling to find my soul
I live struggling to find my identity.
I live a struggle to understand the world
I live a struggle to let the world understand me
I live a struggle to understand myself
I live a struggle to explain myself
I live a struggle to explore my life
I live a struggle to explode my emotions
I live a struggle to understand the reality
I live a struggle to live with true feelings
I live a struggle to live my life without explaining the

crux of living in truth and honesty.
Because living is a lie !!

6. Dilemma

We grow old. We grow bold
We struggle. We juggle
We face obstacles. We overcome obstacles.
We live in pain. We endure the pain.
We reach the end
Yet, we are in a dilemma
To act naive or to act bold
To be insecure or to be confident
To be quiet or to speak out
To keep or to share
Let the dilemma be retained in thoughts
Act bold. Be convinced; speak out.
Share the facts
Be you!! Let the world recognise you !!

7. Ride

Life is an unplanned ride
Ride to the mountains. Ride to the valleys
Ride to the space. Ride to the deep sea
Ride towards the equator. Ride towards the poles
Ride to the north. Ride to the south
Ride to the east. Ride to the west.
Ride to the crowded places. Ride to the secluded places
Ride towards the light. Ride towards the dark.
Ride to the right. Ride to the might.
Ride the soul. Ride the scroll.
Ride in silence. Ride in peace
Ride with twists and turns
Ride with ups and downs
Ride in happiness. Ride in sadness
Ride with tones. Ride with tunes
Live the Ride. Love the Ride. Laugh the Ride
The Ride is a twisted journey, like a curvaceous road to
an unknown destination.
Ride in faith and hope
Planned or unplanned, the Ride is always tedious

Let's make each Ride memorable with everlasting
memories
Live the story of life riding

8. I wish I had

I wish I had the power to control my thoughts
I wish I had the power to control my path
I wish I had the power to control my pain
I wish I had the power to control my claim
I wish I had the power to control my fear
I wish I had the power to control my sphere
I wish I had the power to control my scar
I wish I had the power to control my feelings
I wish I had the power
To rewrite what has been written
To recreate what has been created
To redo what has been done
To change the will of the unwilling.
To redecorate the decorated
To bring back the time that has passed
To rediscover the discovered.
To stay with you, in you, for you,
To see you forever with the same excitement. Same
feeling, same thought, in the same moment
As a twinkle in the eye

The life you have shown
Every moment passed is a memory wished for, to wish
for, and shall wish for.

9. Silenced

Silent because nobody lived like you
Silent because nobody loved like you
Silent because nobody cared like you
Silent because nobody is scarred like you
Silent because nobody is played like you
Silent because nobody has seen you
Silent because nobody understands you.
Silent because nobody knows the battle in you
Silent because nobody knows you
Like the way you know yourself.
The struggle, the juggle, the puzzle, the hustle, the
wrestle to reach the present point in your life
Silent because hoping silence can bring peace
Silent because you were silenced by the pain of living
the life you wished and dreamed

10. Past or Future

Past is no longer my concern
The future is no longer my concern either
You were once my past
Reluctant to be my present
You may be my future
But after all.
This minute is mine to live, love, fight, win
This minute is what matters
To be free, to be loved, to be cared
Live in this minute, laugh in this minute, cry in this
minute
Because life changes with every minute
With it, the battles change
The only positive is that you grow wiser every minute
You can change the outcome of the future by making the
right choices every minute
After all, the past is no longer my concern
The future is no longer my concern either

11. Approachable

How approachable are you??
Does your peer feel you are approachable??
Is that you or your company that is making you
unapproachable??
Is it your circle making you unapproachable??
Is it your vibe making you unapproachable??
Why are you afraid of approaching??
Is it you???
Something is always questionable.
For which you don't have an answer to
You only get accepted by who can approach you !!!
Until then, everyone is a stranger !!!
You cannot change the perceptions of people around you
!!!
It's left to the people around you!!!
Your nature can attract what you can !!!
So live with people who intend to be with you in your
life !!!

12. Today is the memory

Today is the memory
Today is the memory of tomorrow
Every time we cross paths, our brain's chemicals
activate, stimulating memories.
Every time we think about the memory we created, we
realise the reality
Every time we realise the reality, we tend to live in the
old memory, wishing it to be longer
Every time we create, recreate a memory which is either
good, bad or ugly
Life is either lived in created memories or is what we
create every passing moment

13. Occupied

We allow someone into our lives when we are already
occupied
We let someone into our hearts when we are already
preoccupied
We invite someone into our thoughts when we are
already engaged
We open our souls to someone when we are still
occupied

Why do we do all this despite being occupied? In the
end, why do we discard someone as if they were trash?
Life is complicated enough, with so much already
occupying our minds.

When will this " occupied " state become "unoccupied" in
this compelling world?
Yet, life must go on!

14. The beginning or The end

Is it

The beginning of the end or The end of the beginning

Alone in the middle of nowhere

Amidst the storm

A solo sail in the sea

At the edge of the world.

Wishing the beginning to end like it has never begun

Wishing to end the beginning like it has long ended

Catch me if you can say the soul

Finding the space, Exploring the space

Ruling it like no one ever did

Own rules. Own goals. Own claims.

Play. Sway. Make a way.

To the rest to follow

Create a path to destiny

To reach the supreme enlightenment

Lighten the soul. Brighten the life

It is the beginning to the end.

It is the end to the beginning.

15. Journey to Destiny

Is it destiny, or Is it the journey
Life is a journey to destiny
We are bound to the journey
We are bound to the time
We are bound to the companions of the time frame
We are bound to the moments
We are bound to the ever-changing feelings
We are bound to the emotions of life
We are bound to the path of life
We are bound to the journey
We are bound to the boundless journey to destiny
When we are bound to our trip to destiny
Why not create an unbreakable bond
Why not create a life of our own?
Why not create a path filled with joy and happiness
Why not gain experiences to look back at?
Why not live the journey to destiny?
Destiny awaits throughout the journey.
Destiny is never an end paint.

Destiny is the journey we go through and grow through
!!!

16. Fears of truth

What is that you fear??
Haunted by the time that passed
Haunted by the world of conspiracy.
Haunted by the tragic truth
Haunted by the guilt of unexplainability.
Haunted by the unforeseen consequences
Or fearing to face it all ??
Willing to face the fears with strength.
Willing to face the fears with courage.
Willing to face the fears with hope
Willing to face the fears with determination
Willing to face the fears with willpower
Face the fears to succeed beyond expectations.
The world is awaiting your arrival.!!
Plan towards. Act towards
Claim it all. Achieve it all
The world is all that is to achieve!!!

17. Finding yourself

Where are you standing in your life??
Where are you heading towards in your life??
Where were you up with yourself in life??
Every time I recall my life, it is someone else living it.
Every time I recall my life, it is something that stands
ahead of me.
Every time I recall my life, I only sometimes lived up to
myself.
Every time I recall my life, it is pain that I have lived
better than myself.
Every time, it was not me.
I was always the second priority.
It's time to change that someone, something, sometimes,
every time, and to pain that I deserve better than the
rest.
Live life controlling it and not controlled by it !!
I am heading up for the future to find myself more often
than the rest.
Hope keeps me living.
Care, Control, and Conquer yourself before anything else

!!!

You live your life better than anybody can or will !!

Hold up. Gear up. Cheer up life !!!

18. Missed up or Messed up

Life is either missed up or messed up
You either miss something or mess up something in life
To achieve things you think you deserve
You never get to know the missed part if you are not
wise enough
You never get to know the messed part if you feel you
are always right in your thoughts
You will never get to see what you missed or messed up
in life if you never entertain a critic in life
It's not always you have to, but it's always either one of
it
You miss your dream if you wake up from it.
You mess up your dream if you are not practical enough
Life is at a balance of being missed or being messed up
You cannot live without missing.
You can not live without messing up in life.
So live life as it is, not worrying about being missing or
messed up.
You get to where you intend to be even after missing or
messing up many aspects of life.

You ought to embrace missing and messing aspects to live without regrets.!!!

19. Never look back

Never look back at the past
Never look back at the struggles
Never look back at the juggles
Never look back at the fiddles
Never look back at the pain
Never look back at the loss
Never look back at the gain
Never look back at the spent seconds
Never look back at the distance travelled
You can never change anything
All are the steps to eternity.
Life is an ongoing struggle to eternity, bound to time
All the memories will only help
To avoid the mistakes. To avoid the struggles. To avoid
the puddles.
To smile longer and share laughter.
To live gracefully, retire peacefully.
To teach and preach kindness.
Only then you will live limitlessly in this time-limited
journey to eternity.

20. Battle with self

It's scary to team up. It's scary to meet up,
It's scary to partner, and it's scary to start.
Life hasn't been that kind. Life hasn't been in mind.
Scarred by the rocks all through,
Scarred by the mocks all through,
Life hasn't been fonder,
Life still in wandering,
Drawing perimeters one after the other around self-
guarding the delicacy,
Holding onto the perimeters, which are either drawn or
withdrawn with each day,
Life has been this defiant to analyse the mere existence
of rightfulness in thoughts and actions.
The paucity of peacefulness trying to resist all the vibe of
negativity from a distance.
Craving for peace, even in doubt of its existence
Mind is bound to instincts of life and death After being
toppled every single time after an attempt to rise.
This is a battle between being selfish and being selfless

for self.

I hope the conqueror finds lasting peace at last.

21. Into the fog as I walk

Walking into the way
Walking into the way of things
Walking into things on the way.
Walking as I started. Walking as I run.
Walking into the midst of somewhere, I thought I
belonged. Only to learn that it's not where I belong.
Walking into the mist somewhere, I thought I would not
belong, only to learn it's where I might belong.
Walking through the past.
Walking through the present.
Walking through to the future.
Just like the hovered clouds, thuds of the thunder and
the rattling of the rain
Walking through the fog, trying to peep through ahead,
trying to clear the mist, not knowing what's ahead
Walking through the fog in anticipation of the brighter
moments ahead
Walking through the fog as I gear my courage and
resilience to walk through the spine-chilling cold night.
Walking into the fog fondly further into the futuristic

optimism, wishing to see a brighter future filled with
fun, frolicking family and forging myself into a sword
through the fire of ambitions and accomplishments
Into the fog as I walk !!!

www.ingramcontent.com/pod-product-compliance
Lightning Source LLC
Chambersburg PA
CBHW052338150726
47998CB00018B/2473